Mysterious Encounters

Ghost Hunters

by Q.L. Pearce

KIDHAVEN PRESS
A part of Gale, Cengage Learning

GALE
CENGAGE Learning

Detroit • New York • San Francisco • New Haven, Conn • Waterville, Maine • London

LIBRARY OF CONGRESS CATALOGING-IN-PUBLICATION DATA

Pearce, Q. L. (Querida Lee)
  Ghost hunters / by Q.L. Pearce.
    p. cm. -- (Mysterious encounters)
  Includes bibliographical references and index.
  ISBN 978-0-7377-5290-8 (hardcover)
  1. Ghosts--Juvenile literature. I. Title.
  BF1461.P43 2011
  133.1--dc22

                                                    2010034705

KidHaven Press
27500 Drake Rd.
Farmington Hills, MI 48331

ISBN-13: 978-0-7377-5290-8
ISBN-10: 0-7377-5290-4

Printed in the United States of America
1 2 3 4 5 6 7 14 13 12 11 10

Printed by Bang Printing, Brainerd, MN, 1st Ptg., 01/2011

Contents

Chapter 1

The Early Ghost Hunters

Tales of ghosts and haunted houses have been giving people goose bumps for centuries. Two thousand years ago, a Roman senator, named Pliny (PLIN ee) the Younger (A.D. 61–115), told a strange tale he had heard about a haunted house in ancient Athens, Greece.

There was in Athens a house, spacious and open, but with an infamous reputation, as if filled with **pestilence**. For in the dead of night, a noise like the clashing of iron could be heard. And if one listened carefully, it sounded like the rattling of chains. At first the noise seemed to be at a distance, but then it would approach, nearer, nearer, nearer.[1]

According to Pliny, the chains hung from the bony ankles and wrists of an angry ghost. It scared anyone who dared to spend the night. The owner tried to sell the house, but few people even looked at it until a young writer named Athenodorus (uh THEE no dor us) came along. He was not convinced that there was any real danger, so he bought the property. As darkness fell on his first night in the house, Athenodorus settled down to write. Then the noises began. They were faint and distant, but grew louder and closer, until all at once, a ghost appeared in the room. It was the **spirit** of an old man dressed

The spirit of an old man appears to the Greek writer Athenodorus in what is believed to be the first recorded ghost story.

ATHENODORUS CONFRONTS THE SPECTRE.

in rags. His long beard and hair swirled as if they were blown by a **phantom** wind. Moaning and rattling the chains, the ghost loomed over the writer. Unlike others before him, the young Greek did not scream and run. The phantom beckoned with a long bony finger. Athenodorus calmly finished what he was writing, then followed the ghost to the courtyard, where the spirit suddenly vanished. The next morning Athenodorus hired workers to dig up the courtyard. There they found a skeleton bound with chains in a shallow grave. After the body was given a proper burial, the angry spirit was never seen again.

Some modern fans of the **paranormal** say that this tale is the first recorded ghost story, complete with clanking chains and a moaning spirit. Many ghost hunters suggest that it is also the first ghost story in which an investigation took place. Since the time of Athenodorus, tales of hauntings have become common around the world, but true ghost hunters were rare until the middle of the nineteenth century.

Modern Spiritualism

In 1848 two sisters from Hydesville, New York, attracted the attention of the nation. Eleven-year-old Kate and fifteen-year-old Margaretta Fox claimed that they were in contact with the spirit of a dead peddler named Charles Rosma. Their story created great public interest and sparked a popular movement known as **spiritualism**. Followers of the movement believed that the dead could talk with the living through people called **mediums**. The Fox girls said that they were mediums able to connect with Rosma's spirit through a system of knocks and taps. They claimed that he told them he had been murdered in their house, and his body was buried in the basement. Although no body was found and there was no record of a man named Charles Rosma, many people accepted the story. Believers were thrilled to hear proof of life after death. Decades later in 1888, the Fox sisters confessed that they had faked the contact, but the public stayed interested in spirits and hauntings. The sisters' story inspired a small, but dedicated, interest in investigative ghost hunting.

Summoning Spirits

One of the earliest written stories about a medium is found in the Old Testament of the *Bible*. King Saul of Israel was facing a battle and needed the advice of a prophet named Samuel. Because Samuel had died, the king ordered a woman called the Witch of Endor, also known as the Medium of Endor, to call up Samuel's spirit.

Ghost Clubs

The first group to investigate ghosts, the Ghost Club Society, formed in 1851 at England's Cambridge University. In 1862 London's Ghost Club was started. Over time it included many famous poets and authors, such as William Butler Yeats, Charles Dickens, and Sir Arthur Conan Doyle, the author of the Sherlock Holmes mysteries. Members met to talk about ghostly topics and sometimes to **debunk**, or discredit, **charlatans**, or fakes, in the spiritualist movement. The Ghost Club split up after a while, but it formed again in 1882. A new group, the Society for Psychical Research (SPR), began at the same time, and some members belonged to both organizations.

The SPR used science to investigate the paranormal. The Ghost Club was more secret, and its members were more likely to believe in ghosts. In fact, membership in the Ghost Club was forever, so it did not end at death. Every November the names of members, living and dead, were read aloud, and the group believed the ghostly members made their presence felt during this time.

One of the Ghost Club's most controversial members, Harry Price, joined in 1927. In his job as a paranormal investigator, he learned a lot about ghosts and **séances**. Price was good at finding frauds. For example, when a photographer named William Hope made a lot of money by selling pho-

A photograph, taken by William Hope, of a group gathered for a séance. Although the table in the photo appears to be levitating, it was later discovered that the image was faked.

tographs of ghosts, Price proved that Hope had faked the images. The case that made Price a legend was his investigation of a home that was often called the most haunted place in England, the Borley **Rectory**.

England's Most Haunted Home

Borley is a small village not far from the eastern coast of England. The tale of the Borley ghosts began in 1862, when the original owner, the Reverend Henry Bull, built the rectory on land that villagers believed was already haunted. According to a local legend, a **monastery** had once stood on the site. When a monk and a beautiful young nun ran away together, they were caught and killed. The monk was hanged, and the nun was either strangled or buried alive behind a brick wall.

Harry Price during his ghost hunting expedition of the Borley Rectory in England. Although some people consider the haunting of Borley a hoax, others consider Price to be one the first true ghost hunters.

I'm a Believer

According to a survey from October 2008, 34 percent of Americans say they believe in ghosts.

A few months after the rectory was completed, stories of strange events in and around the building began to spread. There were rumors of unexplained footsteps, knocking, ringing bells, and moving objects. The ghosts included a headless man, a woman in white, a phantom nun, and a carriage pulled by a team of ghostly horses. In June 1929 a reporter for the *Daily Mirror* newspaper wrote an article about the paranormal events at Borley. The next day Harry Price received a telephone call from a London editor who asked him to investigate the haunting. Price agreed. He assembled a ghost-hunting team and began an investigation that lasted many years. Price stayed at the rectory several times and said that he witnessed strange things himself.

During his research, Price was the first to use an official ghost-hunter's kit. It included a tape measure to check the thickness of walls, still and motion cameras, thermometers, a fingerprinting kit, and a paranormal investigation handbook, known as *The Blue Book*, which he had written. He even used an early kind of a portable telephone so that the investigators could stay in touch with each other as they moved around the grounds. On the night of March 27, 1938 Price arranged a séance hoping to contact the spirits of the dead. During the séance the medium said that the rectory would burn that very night, and the nun's body would be found among the ruins. The medium's timing was wrong, but the rectory was destroyed by fire in 1939. Witnesses said they saw ghostly figures walking in the flames and the face of a nun watching from an upper window. Later the jaw and skull of a young woman were found in the cellar.

After Price's death some people said that the haunting of Borley Rectory was an elaborate **hoax**. Still, many defend Price's work, and he is considered to be one of the first true ghost hunters.

Chapter 2

Ghostly Encounters

No matter what word is used, a ghost, specter, spirit, apparition, or phantom is something that can be sensed in some way, even though it does not have a solid physical form such as a human body. The definition of a ghost depends on a person's point of view, but most people believe it is the spirit of someone who has died. A ghost may be seen as a hazy or partial figure; heard as whispers, crying, or footsteps; smelled as perfume or smoke; or felt as a change of temperature. Paranormal investigators say there are three common kinds of ghosts: **residual**, active, and noisy ghosts known as **poltergeists** (POLE ter guyst).

Residual Ghosts

Investigators believe that some ghosts may be the leftover energy of someone who once lived. A residual ghost is often seen as a misty figure in old-fashioned clothing. It does not interact with people. It simply repeats an activity that it did when it was

The Whaley House located in San Diego, California, is considered the most haunted house in the United States due to the number of people who died in and around the home even before it was built.

alive, much like a scene from a movie in an endless loop. An example of a residual ghost is found at the Whaley House in San Diego, California.

According to the Travel Channel television show *America's Most Haunted*, the Whaley House is the most haunted house in the United States. Thomas Whaley moved to California during the gold rush in 1849. He built the house a few years later. Over time the home included a theater, a general store, and the County Court House. Today it is a museum. Four Whaley family members died in the house, including Thomas's daughter, Violet, who killed herself.

One of the home's best-known ghosts never lived there. James Robinson, or "Yankee Jim," was a criminal who was hung at the site in 1852, when it was an empty lot. According to a local newspaper, soon after the Whaley family moved into the newly built home in 1857, they reported hearing heavy footsteps at night, such as those made by the boots of a large man. Visitors to the museum say they have seen Yankee Jim and Thomas Whaley himself, dressed in a frock coat and pantaloons. Other guests say that they have seen Thomas's wife, Anna, strolling in the garden. Even the spirit of the family dog, a terrier named Dolly, has been seen on the lower floor. Dolly reportedly licks the legs of visitors wearing shorts. The Whaley House Museum has a monthly tour led by The San Diego Ghost Hunters. Costumed guides carry oil lamps and lead amateur, or beginner, ghost hunters on the late night tour.

Active Ghosts

In an active haunting a ghost appears to be aware of living humans. The ghost might try to get their attention with a soft breath, a push, a tap on the back, or a tug of hair or clothing. Several ghost hunters have said Rolling Hills Asylum in East Bethany, New York, is an active haunt. Built in 1790 as a tavern, the building later housed people in need. It was an orphanage, a nursing home, a home for the criminally insane, and a shopping mall. At one time sick, elderly, and poor inmates lived and ate together in terrible, overcrowded conditions. Close to 1,800 people died on the property, and many are buried there. The building itself is a maze of rooms, hallways, and staircases. Parts have been torn down, and rooms have been added or used for other things. For example, a large meat freezer was once a **morgue**.

A couple bought the property in 2002. It was not long before they knew that something frightening roamed the halls. Visitors said that they saw misty figures and felt touches, pokes, and hair tugs. On a hunt in 2007, a group gathered in a basement room. They sat in a circle in the darkened space with a glow stick, a ball, and a toy rocking horse at the center. Group member Suzie Yencer was chosen to speak to any entity, or being, that might be present.

> The more I talked, the more strange occurrences began to happen. The glow stick started to move back and forth, and the rocking horse began to slowly rock. A few of the guests in the room including myself saw a hand and arm come out of nowhere and reach for the ball in the circle and then just vanish . . . .[2]

Shortly afterward the building closed, but new owners have reopened it for tours. Former owner Lori Carlson states, "In light of the building's history, there exist many unsettled souls wandering the property and within its remaining structures. Is the place really haunted? Many believe so ... but you must find out for yourself."[3]

Poltergeists

The German word *poltergeist* means *noisy ghost*. Things flying across the room, beds shaking, and loud banging may mean these ghosts are around. Poltergeists are not always dangerous. In 1998 Al Cobb of Georgia bought an antique bed for his fourteen-year-old son, Jason. The boy said that when he slept in the bed he felt as if he were being watched. A photo in his room was turned face down every morning, and stuffed toys kept being piled in the center of the bed. Afraid that something unseen was in the room, Jason's father asked that the ghost tell them its name and age, but it did not.

> I left out a sheet of paper and a pen for him to answer me. We all walked out of Jason's room and quietly closed the door behind us. In a moment we returned to find the sheet written on in an eerie childlike stick writ-

Phantom Energy

Centuries ago poltergeist activity was blamed on demons or witchcraft. Modern paranormal investigators think that a poltergeist uses the energy of a living person, often a child.

During this meal in the United Kingdom, poltergeists tip glasses over. Poltergeists are types of ghosts that are associated with the movement of objects and the making of loud noises.

ing, *Danny 7*. I felt a chill in the room and a stronger chill running down my back![4]

Later the ghost wrote that his mother had died in the bed in 1899. The ghost added, *No one sleep in bed*. Jason moved out of the room after a wall hanging flew at him and smashed against the closet door. The trouble spread throughout the house. An unseen hand moved furniture and opened drawers. When paranormal investigators visited, they thought that more than one poltergeist was present. Others said that the activity was mainly due to Jason's **psychic** ability and **electromagnetic energy** in the room.

The Hunters

It is not unusual for ghost hunters to disagree. Some try to prove that a site is haunted. Others, known as debunkers, set out to prove that the site is not haunted. Some **skeptics** think a ghost sighting is a natural happening that has been misunderstood, the result of an overactive imagination, or even a hoax. Ghost hunters usually keep an open mind when investigating sites. They start by looking for natural causes and record what they see and hear. They study the evidence, research the history of the site, talk to witnesses, keep detailed notes, and try to find a balance between belief and skepticism.

Paranormal investigator Joe Nickell is willing to

A ghost hunter from The Atlantic Paranormal Society sets up digital infrared cameras in a suspected haunted location. Modern ghost hunters rely on eyewitness accounts and evidence gathered with cameras and an array of sensors.

check out everything, whether his findings show there is a supernatural explanation or not. He uses skills he learned as a magician, a detective, and a journalist. Nickell says, "I hold that mysteries should neither be fostered nor dismissed. Instead, they should be carefully investigated with a view toward solving them."[5]

In 1972 Nickell investigated the MacKenzie House, home of the first mayor in Toronto, Canada. During the 1960s the caretaker's family reported many ghostly happenings. Footsteps sounded on the empty stairs, spooky piano music echoed through the building at night, and an old printing press clattered in the basement. Nickell began his investigation with the MacKenzie house, but he also talked with the caretaker of the MacMillan Publishing Company warehouse next door.

As it turned out, nightly clean-up crews used an iron staircase in the warehouse. It was less than 2 feet (60.96cm) from the MacKenzie staircase, which explained the late-night footsteps. Nickell also found that the clean-up crew regularly loaded metal garbage cans onto carts, then dragged them across the basement floor. The clatter they made had been mistaken for a ghostly printing press. The MacMillan caretaker also said that he often played the piano in the evening, which may have made the spooky music. Nickell solved many of the mysteries of the MacKenzie House by talking to a witness. Ghost hunters of today use both eyewitness stories and proof they get with cameras and **sensors**.

Chapter 3

Tools and Techniques

G host hunters do not always use expensive tools. The most important tool is good common sense. Still, some equipment and a lot of careful planning make an investigation safer and give better results. Paranormal investigators use many kinds of gear. A camera and tape recorder come in handy, but they do not have to be fancy. Even a disposable camera can do the job.

Phantom Photos

The first spirit photographs were taken in the 1860s. They were spooky images of living people with ghostly figures behind them. These photos were usually fakes made by using tricks such as

Look-alikes

The human brain tends to find familiar images in random patterns. Sometimes people see ghostly faces in photographs that are not really there. The mind sees a face because it wants or expects to. This is called a *simulacrum*, from a Latin word that means *similarity*.

a double exposure. The cameras at that time included a photographic plate that was sensitive to light. When the plate was exposed to the light the image that had been photographed would develop on the plate. By exposing the photographic plate twice, images from two separate photos overlap in a single frame. Modern computer programs such as Photoshop let anyone create a fake ghost image. Still, some ghostly photographs do not look as if they are frauds, or tricks.

On an August afternoon in 1991, members of the Ghost Research Society (GRS) investigated Bachelor's Grove Cemetery near Chicago. The cemetery is more than 150 years old, and gangsters once used it to dump bodies. Witnesses reported more than 100 sightings, including a phantom black dog, misty faces, and a lady in white. In the

A vintage photo showing what appears to be a male ghost. More often than not, these types of ghostly photos were fakes created with tricks such as a double exposure.

1970s two police officers said that they saw a skeletal horse step from the cemetery pond dragging an old man behind it. Once on the bank, the horse and man vanished. The cemetery even has a ghostly house. It is a two-story farmhouse with a porch swing and a light in the window. As someone nears it, the house is said to move farther away. According to a local legend, anyone who enters the house will disappear.

When the ten-member GRS team measured the electromagnetic energy in the area, they found a spot near one tombstone that showed unusual changes in the natural energy field. Ghost hunters say that such changes may occur if a ghost is there. Several team members got a strange feeling at the spot. Paranormal investigators usually take dozens of photographs because something may turn up on film that they did not see with the naked eye. Us-

False Images

Some people say that orbs, or globes, of light in photographs show spirit energy. Ghostly orbs may actually come from spots on the film or reflected light from glass, fog, dust, flying insects, or even a dangling camera strap.

ing a 35-millimeter camera and high-speed infrared film, which captures infrared light that the human eye cannot see, an investigator took several photos of the tombstone. She says that no one was near the stone when she snapped the shots. To everyone's surprise, there was a woman in the photograph wearing a 1920s white dress. Nobody had seen the woman sitting there.

"I know there were several other members at the same time taking photographs of that tombstone with different film, and nobody else got anything," said Dale Kaczmarek, president of GRS. "I can't explain that photograph.... It was one shot out of thirty-six where anything showed up."[6]

Electronic Voice Phenomena (EVP)

Photographs are not the only evidence that ghost hunters collect. Investigators use tape recorders and digital voice recorders to pick up ghostly voices. In January 2007 several members of the Central New York Ghost Hunters (CNYGH) led by Stacey Jones, used recording equipment in an old hotel in upstate New York. The hotel owner let the group stay overnight and set up their equipment as they liked, but asked them not to tell anyone the name of the hotel. The ghost hunters hoped to gather some data, or information. They found much more than they expected.

A ghost hunter participating in an EVP session at the Harmon House in Aurora, Ohio.

Members heard footsteps, voices, and the sound of a phantom cuckoo clock. The most frightening evidence was an **electronic voice phenomena,** or EVP. The unexpected recording was made as two investigators and a member of the owner's family sat together on a hotel staircase. Earlier in the day they had heard what seemed to be muffled voices from an empty upstairs room. The three women settled down and chatted softly as the recorder ran. When they played the lengthy recording back later, they were stunned by what they heard. Below their conversation was a man's voice. An unknown woman said, "Get off me." That was followed by the sounds of the woman being attacked and a long struggle. A male voice said, "Help me" several times. The recording is frightening and difficult to explain. Skeptics point out that EVP voices might come from radio, television, or faulty equipment. They may also be examples of the brain working to find meaning that is not really there or to turn odd sounds into words.

Electromagnetic Field Detectors

Not all investigators use an **electromagnetic field detector** (EMF), but it is often seen on ghost-hunter television shows. The instrument shows natural levels of electromagnetic energy in a given area and can find and track energy sources that cause the levels to fluctuate or change. Such energy sources might be ghosts, but the machine is sensitive, so radio waves, bad electrical wiring, microwave emissions, and even thunderstorms can affect it.

An EMF meter played an unusual part in an investigation in Shokan, New York. The owner of a private home worried that she might be experiencing a haunting, so she contacted The East Coast Ghost Hunters Club (ECGC), founded by Nancy Markert and Virginia Butler. The family living at the home had three young boys, and they all said they had seen paranormal activity. The boys were not afraid of the ghost and, in fact, felt that it watched over them. Their father had not believed them until the day that he went into his youngest son's nursery to wake him from a nap. On the pillow beside the baby was what looked like the deep impression of an adult head.

When the investigators arrived, they sat in the kitchen with the owner to talk about the sightings. Several tools, including two EMF meters, were on the table. As they spoke, the oldest boy, a seven-year-old, began to talk into one of the meters as if it were a two-way radio. The other meter reacted right away, but only when the boy asked a question. The investigators thought that because the two meters were on the table and not being moved, it was unlikely that it was caused by an outside source of

Infrared Thermometers

Temperature changes and cold spots are used to show that a house is haunted. Supposedly, they indicate the presence of a ghost. Investigators use heat sensors, such as digital thermal scanners, to measure temperature changes. Skeptics point out that temperatures can vary throughout a building due to normal causes. For example, there might be a draft from an open door or window, or a room may be colder in certain areas because there is little or no insulation in some areas of the wall.

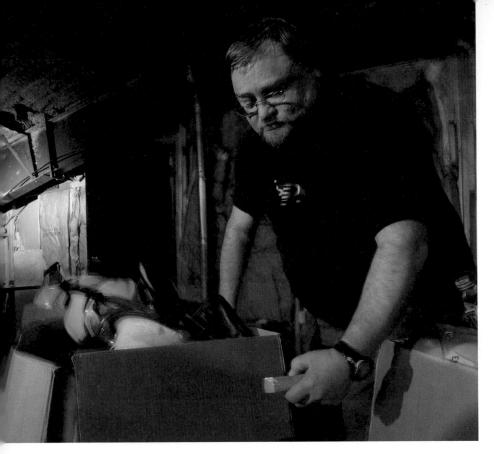

Ghost hunters, like Rusty Edmondson of the Virginia Independent Paranormal Society, commonly use electromagnetic field detectors (EMF) during their investigations in search of paranormal activity.

electromagnetic radiation. The boy asked questions for about fifteen minutes. He spoke each question into one meter. The second meter appeared to pick up the energy of an answer. The team recorded this and took photographs with three different flash cameras. Although the cameras worked fine most of the time, the photos taken during the EMF activity were all black. A picture taken late in the day appeared to show the outline of a face in a window.

The ECGC members decided that there was some evidence of a ghost, but that it was no danger to the family.

The case of the Shokan house showed that ghost hunters may find evidence in ways that they least expect. There are many types of equipment that can come in handy during an investigation, including motion sensors to detect movement within a given area. Air quality monitors show levels of gases, which might cause people to see or hear strange things. Walkie talkies help group members stay in contact with each other. No two researchers are the same, so every ghost hunter's tool kit will contain a different assortment of gear.

Chapter 4

In the Field

Although investigators use many techniques, they agree that a few things are important. Ghost hunters always get permission from the owners or authorities to visit a site. Because haunted places are often isolated and can be dangerous, hunters check the location during the day. They look for hazards, or dangers, that might cause problems later, because most hunts are done in darkness. Author Tom Ogden notes, "Historically, the most active times for ghost phenomena are between 9 P.M. and 6 A.M."[7] Even so, hauntings may happen any time of day or night, and they may happen in many different types of places.

Before investigating the old Beauregard Parish Jail in DeRidder, Louisiana, the group Louisiana Spirits, pictured here, requested permission from authorities to tour the facility. Ghost hunters all agree that permission should be sought before the start of an investigation.

Hot Spots

Ghost hunters regularly investigate haunted houses, but they visit other places too. Phantom activity is often reported in theaters, schools, hotels, and particularly in places where suffering has occurred, such as hospitals and prisons. It is also logical to look for ghosts in a cemetery where people are buried. The place that fills the number one spot on *Haunted America's* list of top ten most haunted cemeteries is the St. Louis No. 1 in New Orleans.

Established in 1789, it is the oldest cemetery in the city. Before modern drainage was used, the ground in New Orleans held so much water that coffins that were buried would slowly float back up to the surface, so St. Louis No. 1 is a maze of above-ground **crypts** and narrow, winding paths. Some visitors have heard crying and moaning from inside the tombs. Others have seen swirling mists and transparent figures. Many famous people are buried at the site, including the Voodoo Queen of New Orleans, Marie Laveau, who was well known

Guidelines for a Safe Ghost Hunt

- Do not ghost hunt alone. Always go with a team.
- Wear sturdy shoes and comfortable clothing.
- Carry a working flashlight and cell phone.
- Check the site during daytime hours for hazards.
- Get permission from the owner to be at the site.
- If a member of the team becomes very frightened, leave.

St. Louis No. 1 cemetery in New Orleans is the number one spot on *Haunted America's* list of top ten most haunted cemeteries and home to the grave of Marie Laveau, Voodoo Queen and paranormal practitioner.

for her involvement with the paranormal. There are daily historical and ghost tours at St. Louis No. 1. Investigators say that it is important to be respectful when visiting any cemetery. People might be visiting loved ones who are buried there and their feelings must be considered. Also, noisy or disrespectful guests might be asked to leave the grounds. Most burial sites are on private property, and they can be hazardous at night. Only the most experienced teams of ghost hunters visit cemeteries after dark, and they try to do a thorough walk-through of the site during daylight hours.

Sites of Sadness

It is often said that ghosts are the spirits of people who died tragically. The Waverly Hills Sanatorium in Kentucky was built for patients who had the deadly lung disease, tuberculosis. The hilltop hospital opened in 1910 and closed in 1961. In that time as many as 10,000 patients or more may have died there. The bodies were taken away in carts through an underground tunnel that came to be called the "Body Chute." The doctors thought it would be better if the living patients did not see the dead, and they hoped it would prevent further spread of the disease. After the development of antibiotics, the hospital was no longer needed.

Over the years people have reported seeing a little girl on the third-floor stairs and looking down from a third-floor window. One witness said the girl had no eyes. There are frightening stories about a woman with bleeding wrists calling for help, a hearse dropping off coffins, and a ring of children on the roof chanting the child's poem "Ring Around the Rosie."

A March 2006 episode of the Syfy [formerly Sci-Fi] Channel television show *Ghost Hunters* showed an investigation of Waverly Hills. A team from The Atlantic Paranormal Society (TAPS) inspected the infamous room 502, where a nurse was said to have killed herself and found nothing unusual. Most visitors say that they feel very uncomfortable in the room. Marty Seibel and a team from the Shenandoah Valley Paranormal Society explored the hospital in August 2008. He says,

> Once we began to analyze our data, we found we collected some fantastic evidence ranging from many EVPs to personal experiences … we found out that Waverly was actually very active that night. Bottom line, we believe Waverly Hills is haunted, very haunted! If you have the opportunity to investigate the hospital, by all means do it![8]

Alcatraz Island in San Francisco Bay is the site

of one of the most famous prisons in the world. Early Native Americans believed the island was an evil place. Alcatraz began as a military prison, then served as a federal prison from 1934 to 1963. Today it is a part of the National Park Service, and it can be reached by ferryboat. Visitors report hearing crying, moaning, gunshots, and screams as well as the feeling of being watched. The most haunted area on Alcatraz is Cellblock D. Because the prisoners there were often violent, they were kept apart from other prisoners. They ate meals alone in their cells, which were terribly cold. Cells 9 to 14 had no windows and one dim lightbulb. Those cells were for prisoners who caused trouble, and there were rumors of an angry phantom that occupied those cells.

According to one story, a prisoner who was locked into cell 14-D began to scream that someone with glowing eyes was in it with him. The guards

A cell in Alcatraz's Cellblock D, considered by some to be the most haunted area of the prison. Rumors suggest that an angry phantom occupies the cells of this area.

ignored him until the screaming stopped. When they finally checked on the man, he was dead and had handprints on his throat. Several guides who conduct tours at Alcatraz have said that there are strong feelings associated with cell 14-D, and, no matter how hot the day is, inside that cell it is always cold. In the fall of 1981, ghost hunter Richard Senate spent the night on Alcatraz as part of a radio promotion. He locked himself in cell 12-D and reported that, when the steel door was closed, he felt icy fingers on his neck. He knew he was not alone.

Hunting for the Truth

Do ghosts really exist? Do those footsteps in the night have a logical explanation or are they caused by something sinister? Although most people avoid spooky houses and haunted hotel rooms, ghost hunters seek them out. The answers may not always be clear, but one thing is certain. When it comes to hauntings, ghost hunters will be there to shine a light in the darkest corners.

Notes

Chapter 1: The Early Ghost Hunters

1. Pliny the Younger, from the *Letters of Pliny the Younger* originally translated by William Melmoth (1710–1799). Quoted in "An Ancient Ghost Story," *The Nostalgia League: The Library*. Available online at http://thenostalgialeague.com/olmag/ghost_story.htm.

Chapter 2: Ghostly Encounters

2. Quoted in Stephen Wagner, "Rolling Hills Asylum, E. Bethany, New York," *About.com Guide*. Available online at http://paranormal.about.com/od/hauntedplaces/ig/World-s-Most-Haunted-Place/Rolling-Hills-Asylum.htm.

3. Quoted in Gina Keller (case manager), "Rolling Hills," *NYX Paranormal Research Investigation Team*, June 19, 2009. Available online at http://www.paranormalnyx.com/rollinghills-1.html.

4. Al Cobb, "The Open Vault First-Hand Paranormal Reports: Danny 7," *X-Project Paranormal Magazine, Archives 1997–2006*, (September 1998). Available online at http://www.xprojectmagazine.com/openvault/danny7.html.

5. Joe Nickell, "Paranormal Investigator," *JoeNickell.com*, 2010. Available online at http://www.joenickell.com/ParanormalInvestigator/paranormalinvestigator1.html.

Chapter 3: Tools and Techniques

6. Quoted in Chris Laursen, "Bachelor's Grove Seeks Single White Apparition," *Bachelors Grove Cemetery & Settlement Research Center,* March 7, 2007. Available online at http://www.bachelorsgrove.com/webzines/751-bachelors-grove-seeks-single-white-apparition.html.

Chapter 4: In the Field

7. Tom Ogden, *The Complete Idiot's Guide to Ghosts and Haunting.* New York: Alpha Publishing, 1999, p. 132.
8. Marty Seibel, "Investigation #017: Waverly Hills Sanatorium, Louisville, KY," *Shenandoah Valley Paranormal Society,* August 3, 2008. Available online at http://www.valleyghosthunters.com/waverly.htm.

Glossary

charlatans: People who falsely claim to have a skill or knowledge.

crypts: Underground burial chambers.

debunk: To expose false claims usually by ridicule and mockery.

electromagnetic energy: A type of energy that involves electricity and magnetism. Some examples of electromagnetic energy include radio waves, infrared radiation, and X-rays.

electromagnetic field detector: A machine that shows changes in electromagnetic energy.

electronic voice phenomena: A voice on tape that can be heard when the tape is played back, but not as it is recorded.

hoax: A plan or plot that tricks others.

mediums: Persons who are able to communicate directly with spirits.

monastery: A place where a community of people, usually, monks live together according to their religious vows.

morgue: A room or building where dead bodies are kept before burial.

paranormal: Something that cannot be explained or understood by science.

pestilence: Serious or deadly disease.

phantom: Something that can be seen, heard, or felt, but that has no body.

poltergeists: Entities that usually reveal their presence with noise or disturbances.

psychic: Someone who is sensitive to supernatural or non-physical influences.

rectory: A house where a priest, preacher, or parson lives.

residual: Used to describe something that is left over or left behind.

séance: A meeting at which a medium talks with spirits.

sensors: Machines that show changes in movement or temperature.

skeptics: People who question or doubt the truth of things that others accept.

spirit: A supernatural being that does not have a body.

spiritualism: A belief that the dead can talk to the living through a person known as a medium.

For Further Exploration

Books

William W. Lace, *Ghost Hunters (The Library of Ghosts & Hauntings)*. San Diego, CA: Reference-Point Press, 2010. There are lots of sidebars and photographs in this overview of paranormal investigators.

Marc Tyler Nobleman, *Detective Notebook: Ghost Hunting Handbook*. New York: Sterling, 2007. An overview of ghosts, including where and when to find them and how to record supernatural encounters.

Jason Rich, *The Everything Ghost Book: Spooky Stories of Haunted Houses, Phantom Spirits, Unexplained Mysteries, and More*. Avon, MA: Adams Media, 2001. This book includes stories; a list of haunted inns, hotels, and historic places; and tips on the best ways to detect and expose a ghostly hoax.

Michael Teitelbaum, *Ghosts: And Real-Life Ghost Hunters (24/7: Science Behind the Scenes)*. Chicago: Children's Press, 2008. Explores the science of ghosts and ghost hunting.

Web Sites

Ghost Hunters Headquarters (http://www.syfy .com/ghosthunters/). This is the official site for the Syfy series, *Ghost Hunters*. It includes stories, how-to's, episodes, and great links.

Kids.Ghostvillage.com (http://kids.ghostvillage .com/). A site just for kids that includes Ghosts in the Classroom, Information for Junior Ghost Hunters, and Professor Perry J. Normal's blog.

The Shadowlands (http://theshadowlands.net/ ghost/). This site has a lot about everything ghostly including ghost stories, ghost-hunting tips, lists of haunted places, and lists of ghost-hunting groups.

Index

Picture Credits

About the Author

Q. L. Pearce has written more than one hundred trade books for children and more than thirty classroom workbooks and teacher manuals on the topics of reading, science, math, and values. Pearce has written science-related articles for magazines; regularly gives presentations at schools, bookstores, and libraries; and is a frequent contributor to the educational program of the Los Angeles County Fair. She is an Assistant Regional Advisor for The Society of Children's Book Writers and Illustrators.